Ripley's Believe It or Not!

Developed and produced by Ripley Publishing Ltd

This edition published and distributed by:
Mason Crest Publishers Inc.
370 Reed Road, Broomall, Pennsylvania 19008
(866) MCP-BOOK (toll free)
www.masoncrest.com

Ripley's Believe It or Not!
Animal Antics
ISBN 978-1-4222-1535-7
Library of Congress Cataloging-in-Publication data is available

Ripley's Believe It or Not!—Complete 16 Title Series
ISBN 978-1-4222-1529-6

PUBLISHER'S NOTE
While every effort has been made to verify the accuracy of the entries in this book,
the Publishers cannot be held responsible for any errors contained in the work.
They would be glad to receive any information from readers.

WARNING
Some of the stunts and activities in this book are undertaken by experts and should not
be attempted by anyone without adequate training and supervision.

Printed in the United States of America

ANIMAL ANTICS

PUBLISHING

a Jim Pattison Company

Animal Antics

Packed full of outrageous animals, read about the

basset hound with extraordinarily long ears that

measure a whopping 13 in (33 cm), the piglet who

knows two heads are better than one, and, believe

it or not—a squirrel that can actually water-ski!

*When buried up to your
chin in worms, why not try
eating your way out...*

It's a Dog's Life

YOU MAY THINK that luxury is the sole preserve of humankind, but you'd be wrong.

Now your pets can be treated to exactly the same kind of pampering as you. You can even treat them to such delights as a night in a top-quality hotel, at which they can experience a hot-spring treatment!

A hotel in Paris, France, has taken customer service to the next level. The hotel staff are all specially trained to deliver the highest-quality food and service to pets!

Pampered Pooch

Jasper, a black Doberman-Labrador, travels by stretch limo and owns stocks and shares worth $194,000 (£130,000). The dog, who lives with his owner, Sir Benjamin Slade, in Somerset, England, also enjoys a daily menu of sirloin steak, Dover sole, and New Zealand freshwater mussels.

TOP FIVE
DOG TALES

1. An estimated 1 million dogs in the U.S.A. have been named primary beneficiary in their owners' wills

2. Every dog except the chow has a pink tongue—the chow's tongue is jet black

3. Sumo, a Neapolitan mastiff, was evicted from his owner's flat in Romania in 2004 because neighbors complained that he snored too loudly

4. Each year, parks in London, England, are soaked in 1 million gal (4.5 million l) of dog urine

5. When Ella Wendel of New York died in 1931, she left $75 million to her poodle, Toby

Four-paw-ster
Who couldn't get a good night's sleep in a luxury four-poster bed? Evie was a lucky enough dog to spend the night in one of designer Jane Evans' luxurious bespoke doggy beds.

Bark-itecture
This state-of-the-art dog kennel, designed by architect Lisa Vogt, sold for $9,200 when it was auctioned for charity in Florida in 2004.

Chipmunk Cheek
When Charlie the chipmunk decided he was thirsty, a long, cool glass of freshly squeezed orange juice didn't last very long. Charlie deftly sucks on the straw before diving head-first into the glass and gulping the lot!

High Steaks

When Romanian health officials investigated a strange smell coming from the home of Gyenge Lajos, they discovered that the 74-year-old was storing a dead cow in his living room! Apparently he had been given the animal by a friend and carved and cooked strips of the rotting corpse when he felt hungry.

Feline Romantic

In 1996, two rare "diamond-eyed" cats called Phet and Ploy were married in a Thai disco. The event cost $16,241.

This Bone's Chewy

If your dog's breath is causing offense, you need to give your pooch chewing gum for dogs. The gum, which is made by the Brazilian company Chiclet, looks like a bone and is made from edible leather.

Oh Deer

You might be surprised to learn that the most dangerous animals at large in the U.S.A. are not bears, sharks, poisonous snakes, or even spiders—but deer. The mild-mannered mammals are responsible for the deaths of about 100 people every year because they often cause road accidents. Bees, dogs, rattlesnakes, and spiders also rank among the top five killers of the animal world.

Best-dressed Crab

First held in 1975, the Miss Crustacean Hermit-crab Beauty Contest draws hundreds of enthusiasts to the beach at Ocean City, New Jersey, for the search to find the best-dressed crab. The winner receives the Cucumber Rind Cup, and past entries have included Cleopatra Crab and Crabzilla.

Monkey Business

Declaring that he wanted to be "at one with the monkeys," 32-year-old Peter Vetique stripped down to his boxer shorts, scaled a 20-ft (6-m) high fence and jumped into the gorilla enclosure at New York's Bronx Zoo in 2001.

Lounge Lizards

In 2002, police called to a man's apartment in Newark, Delaware, after he had failed to report for work, found his body on the floor... and his pet Nile monitor lizards feeding on his flesh.

Cats, dogs, gerbils, guinea pigs, parakeets, and a tortoise were among the congregation at the 2003 Blessing of the Animals' service at Saint Philip's in the Hills Episcopal Church, Tucson, Arizona. Hundreds of owners and their pets gathered for the service, which went off peacefully apart from a Beagle barking during prayers.

Suite Talk

A pet hotel in Fairfax County, Virginia, charges $230 for a dog's use of a hydrotherapy pool, state-of-the-art exercise room, beauty parlor, and suites with satellite TV and classical music.

When Marilyn, a Doberman Pinscher, ran away from her new home in Sault Ste Marie, Ontario, in 2002, owners Ron and Peggy Lund lured her back using a borrowed kitten. The dog adores kittens and was powerless to resist the plaintive miaowing.

Commemorating a story about a chicken from the 1940s that allegedly lived for 18 monthsafter having its head chopped off, the town of Fruita, Colorado, holds an annual "Mike the Headless Chicken Day." Events include the 3 mi (4.8 km) "Run Like a Headless Chicken Race," egg tosses, "Pin the Head on the Chicken," "Chicken Bingo," and the classic "Chicken Dance."

Some of the priciest pets coveted by Americans cost more than a luxury car. For instance, a lavender albino ball python will set you back approximately $40,000, a striped ball python will cost you $20,000, and a reticulated albino tiger python costs $15,000.

On the Couch
Pam Whyte, a canine therapist from Cape Town, South Africa, has a consultation with a collie.

Dog Spa
A hot spring in Tokyo, Japan, has shelled out on a new annex—designed especially for dogs! For as little as $25, pets can enjoy a hot tub filled with volcanic waters, before retiring to a luxury room for a dog nap.

Poodle Power

Palm Beach County, Florida, the scene of voting controversy during the 2000 presidential election, was at the eye of a fresh electoral row in 2001, when it emerged that Cocoa Fernandez was registered to vote. The problem was, Cocoa was a poodle belonging to 62-year-old Wendy Albert.

Snake in the Grass

A New Jersey man tried to steal two pythons and was bitten for his actions. The 20-year-old thief managed to slip the snakes out of a pet store in canvas bags attached to his pants. But on the drive home one of the snakes wrapped around the man's leg and latched on to his groin.

The Hitcher

A Russian Blue/ Angora cross-bred cat by the name of Tracker went on an unplanned 150-mi (240-km) ride from Kalamazoo to Rochester Hills, Michigan, when Patricia Verduin, a college student, drove home for Christmas. Despite traveling under the hood, Tracker didn't seem harmed by the experience.

To Dye For...

Coloring your hair is no longer the preserve of humans. A pet grooming parlour in Chongqing, China, has started to offer services for pets including haircut and color.

Building up his Mussels

A Purdue University professor has discovered how mussels stick themselves to surfaces: they attach tiny filaments to objects that act like glue. He believes that this mussel "glue" could be used commercially in the future, perhaps in sealing wounds or in nerve reconstruction.

Fir Goodness' Sake

For some reason, a dog in Denver, Colorado, scampered 30 ft (9 m) up a blue spruce tree. Amused city workers had to enlist the services of a cherry-picker to bring the poor pooch down to earth.

The Great Escape

Red is one cunning dog, but kennel owners hope his jail breaks are a thing of the past. Red's expertise, it seems, is breaking out of his cage at Battersea Dogs' Home, London, England, for midnight raids on the kitchen—and freeing the other dogs to join him. Having observed Red's technique on video, staff have added extra security devices to his kennel.

MoRe ThaN You CaN Chew

A **50-LB (23-KG) FLATHEAD** catfish had to be rescued after it playfully grabbed a basketball— and got it stuck in its mouth!

The catfish wrapped its jaws around the basketball, which was floating in the water, but the ball got stuck in the fish's tight grip. Pam and Bill Driver, from Wichita, Kansas, saw that the fish was in trouble and could not swim freely with the ball wedged in its mouth, and they began a brave rescue attempt.

It becomes clear to the Drivers that the catfish is in need of help, so Bill goes to the aid of the fish and gets into the water.

The ball is jammed so tightly into the catfish's mouth that it's a struggle to remove it— but it has to be done to allow the fish to swim freely again.

Bill finally manages to get hold of the catfish and pull the basketball from its tight grip.

Crocodile Priority

Patients waiting for ultrasound treatment at a hospital in Croatia were kept waiting for hours after a doctor took his 4-ft (1.2-m) pet crocodile for a check-up.

Milking it

This 1928 statue commemorates the world's champion milk-producing cow—it produced 3,739 gal (16,997 l) of milk in one of its record-beating years! It also produced 2,865 lb (1,300 kg) of butter. You can see just how many milk bottles would have been needed to contain all the milk.

Sonic Saviors

Dolphin researcher Dr. Michael Hyson says that dolphins can generate sound and electromagnetic fields that may be able to help treat human diseases. He believes they have something to contribute in the treatment of conditions such as autism, cerebral palsy, and depression. Speaking from experience, he says that a dolphin helped to heal a couple of painful dislocated vertebrae in his own back when he went swimming with the creature.

Party Animal

In 2004, British pet-lover Jan Einzig threw a champagne party at a top London club for her West Highland terrier Gucci. To date, she has also spent more than $18,000 (£12,000) on vet's bills for treatments for the ailing dog.

Insect-lover

A lonely widower in Beijing, China, kept some 200,000 cockroaches in his home as pets. He began breeding them following the death of his wife.

Flight of Fancy

American entrepreneurs Mark and Lorraine Moore have been raking in big bucks by selling bird diapers through their company, the appropriately titled Avian Fashions. The Lycra suits, which cost between $20 and $26, allow pet birds to roam freely around their owner's house without soiling the furniture—that is as long as the pads are changed every six hours. The Moores say that their friends and family initially thought the idea was rather "flighty."

Champion Chimp

Animals can be just as creative us humans. You only have to look at the works of art produced by Asuka, a three-year-old chimpanzee, who made her debut in the art world when she exhibited 50 of her paintings in Tokyo in 2004.

Cat People

A Georgia couple adopted 77 cats, with the Humane Society's blessing, because they take such good care of them. All of the felines are healthy, well fed, and given access to lots and lots of litter boxes. The couple go through 60 lb (27 kg) of cat litter each week.

Fat Chance

Pumpkin, who weighed 12 lb (5 kg), was certainly one chubby Chihuahua. Her Florida owner took her to the local veterinary surgeon for a little liposuction, where they removed 12 oz (340 g) of fat. However, the surgeon reminded Pumpkin's owner that in order to stay svelte, the pooch really needed to take regular exercise and wolf down fewer treats.

Café Society

The Meow Mix Café opened on Fifth Avenue in New York City in 2004. The cat clientele are offered various different Meow Mix varieties. Alternatives to cat food are available for their owners.

Do You Take Amex?

Her Highness Princess Zarina Zainal of Malaysia thinks nothing of traveling halfway around the globe to visit the vet with her 16-year-old Yorkshire terrier, Amex. Every trip involves a 14-hour flight from Bangkok to Paris, followed by a seven-hour flight from Paris to New York, and then a two-hour drive to the vet's office in South Salem, New York.

Playful Pigs

Pigs were taught to play video games and hit targets and match objects, using their snouts to control the joysticks. The feat was set-up and recorded by Prof. Curtis at Pennsylvania State University. Rewards came in the form of candies.

Ear, Ear

Jack, a two-year-old Basset-hound, has ears that measure a whopping 13 in (33 cm) in length! Jack's ears are insured for $50,000.

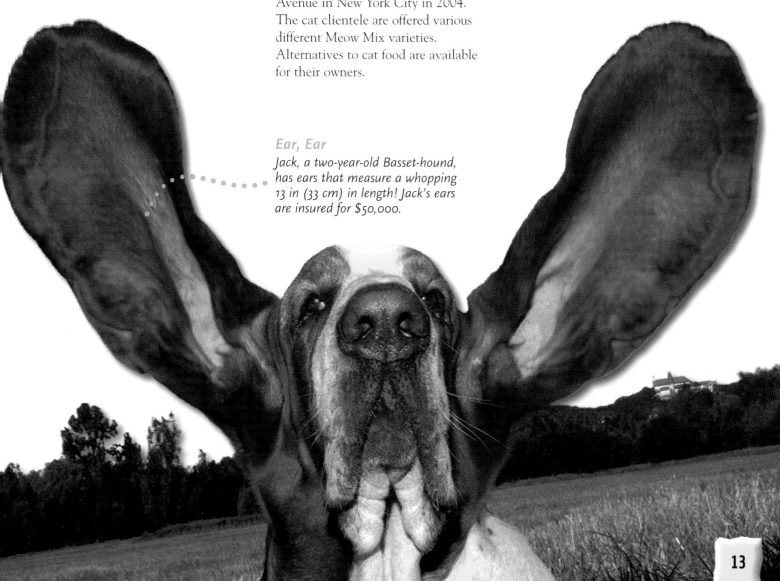

Honey Bunch

Steve Conlon runs a honey business in West Virginia. The honey-bees join in Steve's unusual party piece: Wearing a living "beard" of about 10,000 bees on his face!

Trick or Treat?

Michele Carlin of Michigan sells Halloween costumes for dogs from her store, the Puppy Boutique. She takes her own Yorkshire terrier and Schnauzer trick-or-treating, and encourages others to do the same.

The Importance of Being Ernest's

About 60 cats live at the Ernest Hemingway Home and Museum in Key West, Florida. Most are descended from Hemingway's pet cat, Princess Six Toes.

All the Presidents' Pets

The Presidential Pet Museum in Maryland, just 20 mi (30 km) from the White House, has more than 500 items related to the pets of past presidents.

Bear-faced Cheek

Juan, an Andean spectacled bear, made a dramatic bid for freedom at Germany's Berlin Zoo in August 2004. First he paddled across a moat using a log as a raft, then he scaled the wall of his enclosure. Bizarrely, he looked to complete his getaway on a bicycle, which he found standing against the zoo railings. Before he could climb onto the saddle, he was cornered by zoo-keepers wielding brooms, and immobilized with a tranquilizer dart.

Giddy Up

Whiplash the monkey is a rodeo act with a difference—he rode in a tiny saddle on the back of a collie to herd sheep at the annual Calgary Stampede in Alberta, Canada.

Doggy-vision

German police who were responding to a complaint about excessively loud noise had to force their way into a house when no one answered the door. They were surprised to find Bruno the Alsatian cross-breed sitting on the couch with his paw on the television's remote control.

Sign Here, Please

Rin Tin Tin, a German Shepherd, was Hollywood's first canine star. He starred in 27 movies, always signing his contracts with paw prints. His death in 1932 made front-page news.

Packing a Punch

George W. Bush's pet Scottish Terrier appeared in a spoof political video during the campaign trail for the 2004 election. Barney the dog was shown dressed in a headband and barking at Jon Kerry's dog, with the theme from the *Rocky* films playing as background music.

Marked From Birth

Why, it's a Goldfish
This goldfish, which grew up in an aquarium in Taipei, China, has birth markings of a question mark on its face.

IN AUGUST 2003, an eight-year-old boy made a happy discovery as he walked along a beach in Mie Prefecture, Japan—a crab with a smiley face on its shell!

This species of crab, ironically called *Gaetice depressus*, has a shell that measures about 0.6 in (1.5 cm) across. The crab's "happy" markings struck the boy who discovered it as so unusual that he presented it to Japan's Toba Aquarium.

Staff at Japan's Toba Aquarium initially thought this crab's happy face must have been drawn on with a permanent marker.

Full of Heart
In the 1930s, Weaver Blake of Kansas owned a very special horse named Sweetheart. The horse had a heart-shaped birthmark clearly visible on its hide.

Seventh Heaven

There have been many animals that have been born with clear birthmarks of numbers, but none so lucky as those with "7" on their skin. Robert Ripley received dozens of photographs from people who owned calves born with perfect "7s" on their foreheads.

Ready Meal

"Buck" Fulford claimed an astonishing feat by killing, plucking, cooking, and eating a chicken in 1 minute 50 seconds. His method? He held the chicken upside-down and cut off its head, allowing 40 seconds for it to die, 10 seconds for scalding, 5 seconds to remove feathers, cut out its entrails, and cut it into four portions, dropped it into boiling fat for 30 seconds, then placed it in cracked ice for a further 25 seconds!

Take a Pew

The St. Francis Episcopal Church in Stamford, Connecticut, provides special church services, and even Holy Communion, for pets.

Parrot Fashion

A Congo African Gray parrot called N'Kisi, owned by Aimee Morgana of Manhattan, has astonished the scientific world with its vocabulary of more than 700 words. It has also impressed others with its accurate use of tenses of verbs, its keen sense of humor, and even its telepathic abilities.

When it Comes to the Crunch

In a divorce settlement in Edmonton, Canada, Kenneth Duncan was ordered to pay his ex-wife $200 every month in dog support. On top of that, he also had to dig deep to fund a $2,000 retroactive payment for the care of their St. Bernard, Crunchy.

Silver Service

English eccentric Francis Henry Egerton, the eighth Earl of Bridgwater, had 12 dogs that ate with him every day at formal dinners. The dogs were served from silver dishes.

Married to the Mutt

A nine-year-old Indian girl, Karnamoni Handsa, married a dog in order to ward off an evil omen. Village elders said she would be free to marry a man when she was older, and wouldn't need a divorce from the dog.

Emergency Service

Firefighters in Florida have oxygen masks to help anyone who might have inhaled smoke… including pets. They carry masks for cats, dogs, and even hamsters.

On the Double

This piglet, born in China in 2002, had two heads and three eyes.

Dressed up to the Canines!

The annual ten-day Fantasy Fest held in Key West, Florida, is a chance for everyone to get dressed up and have some fun. It's not just humans who get to join in—pets from across the U.S.A. come to compete in the Pet Masquerade and Parade. Events include the Pet/Owner Look-alike competition, in which owners and pets dress in matching outfits to suit their chosen theme—ranging from historical figures, such as Marie Antoinette, to sports, such as scuba-diving.

Peri Stone and her pet Woody entered in 2002, using The Beatles' "Yellow Submarine" as their theme.

"Miss Trouble," a five-year-old Mexican green iguana entered the Pet/Owner Look-alike competition in the 2000 Fantasy Fest. Her owner, Todd Heins, took the contest very seriously and did a convincing job of making himself up to resemble his beloved reptile.

Piggy in the Middle

A Bengal tiger called Saimai was suckled by a sow and grew up with a litter of piglets. The unusual family lives peacefully at the Si Racha tiger farm in Thailand.

Pump up the Volume

Serbian farmers have found a secret weapon to help deter the wild boars that destroy their crops: Loud rock music. People play it at full volume to scare away their porcine visitors— apparently Meatloaf has proven especially effective.

Unscheduled Departure

Billy the cat was put on to a flight from Phoenix, Arizona, bound for Philadelphia, where he was due to transfer to a connecting international flight. Billy somehow managed to escape from his cage and ended up stuck in the plane's cargo hold for 19 days. Eventually, the cat was discovered at Manchester Airport in New Hampshire, and finally reunited with his owners.

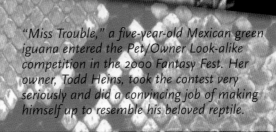

Making a Splash

Grey squirrels are renowned for their athleticism, but Twiggy can do more than just climb trees. Under the watchful eye of Florida trainer Lou Ann Best, Twiggy demonstrates her skills as a water-skier at boat shows across America. Twiggy is towed around a 6-in (15-cm) deep inflatable pool at speeds of up to 6 mph (10 km/h) by a remote-controlled model boat. Lou Ann says the key to training Twiggy is affection, patience—and plenty of nuts.

Only the Best

Pigs, cats, monkeys, and even horses are permitted to fly on U.S. airlines—but only in first class.

Finders Keepers

A Cincinnati couple paid a $10,000 reward to a man who found their dog after it had gone missing.

Animal Hospital

An injured labrador made its own way to Beckley Appalachian Regional Hospital in West Virginia after it had been hit by a car.

The Downward Dog

A chain of gyms in the U.S.A. offers yoga classes specially designed for dogs and their owners, claiming that the exercise reduces the levels of canine stress.

Litter Bugs

The Feline Evolution CatSeat is a toilet seat for cats, which is mounted on a regular toilet. Apparently it takes two to three weeks for a cat to get used to it.

Going the Whole Hog

Anne Langton of Derbyshire, England, holds the world record for the largest collection of pig-related objects. She owns more than 10,000 porcine knick-knacks, including piggy banks, teapots, kettles, and plush toys.

Speeding Bill

In 2002, a traffic radar camera in northern Germany caught a speeding duck. The bird must have been flying fast to set off the radar system, but a precise speed could not be determined.

Two Heads are Better than One

Trixie, a blue-tongued lizard with two heads, was discovered in Australia.

Speed Limit

The peregrine falcon is the world's fastest living creature. The birds can reach speeds of between 124 mph (200 km/h) and 168 mph (270 km/h) when swooping from great heights or while catching birds in mid-air.

Paws for Thought

Most cats have five toes on each paw, but Robert Ripley documented many cases of multi-toed cats. One, Whitney, who lived with his owner in New York, had as many as 32 toes—eight on each paw!

Cool Mules

Mule Day, a four-day celebration of the humble mule, is held every year in Columbia, Tennessee. Thousands of visitors come from far and wide to attend the festivities, which include mule shows, arts and crafts booths, and a parade.

Switched On

Monique Cadonic thinks that her male cat, Lincoln, a Russian Blue cross, might just be trying to communicate something. Lincoln appears to take great pleasure in batting light switches on and off—particularly when Monique's husband has just got into the shower.

Shaggy Sheep Story

Shrek, a runaway merino ram who was loose for six years in New Zealand, was finally caught by shepherds after surviving several harsh winters. His huge fleece was so overgrown that it weighed 60 lb (27 kg). He was finally shorn by former blade-shearing world champion Peter Casserly—in a speedy 20 minutes! Shrek's fleece was later auctioned for a children's charity.

WoRm His Way OuT

BURIED UP TO his chin in more than 10,000 earthworms, Mark Hogg wormed his way out by actually eating some of them!

Survivalist Mark was gradually buried in the earthworms, then proceeded to eat them—without using his hands—for a whole hour.

That's a whole lot of worms!

Two Ripley employees started to load up the container around Mark.

Keep 'em coming.

Once buried, he was watched by eager spectators as he started to eat.

One of the Family

Maddy, a three-year-old chocolate Labrador Retriever, knows just how much her owner loves her because, without the slightest hesitation, he gave her mouth-to-mouth resuscitation. When Maddy got into difficulties in a river, her owner dived in to save her. He then compressed her chest and blew air into her mouth as he performed CPR. He says that's just what you do for family members.

Law and Order

The black squirrels of Council Bluffs, Iowa, are protected by a law that says that people must not "annoy, worry, maim, injure, or kill" any of them.

Slippery Customer

Pulling a snake through your nose and out of your mouth is not everyone's idea of fun, but this man in Madras, India, made a feat of it. He also swallowed 200 worms in 20.22 seconds!

KITTY KAPERS

- 95 per cent of cat-owners admit to talking to their cats
- A cat can jump up to seven times its own height
- A cat can't see directly under its own nose
- A 15-year-old cat has probably spent ten years of its life asleep
- Americans spend more on cat food than on baby food
- The Russian blue cat often has an extra toe
- Cat urine glows under a black light
- Cats have more than 100 vocal sounds; dogs have about ten
- A Texan tabby cat named Dusty gave birth to 420 kittens during her life

Two of a Kind

Scientists in Texas successfully cloned a cat for the first time on December 22, 2001. Rather surprisingly, the aptly named CopyCat owes its existence to a rich dog-lover, Dr. John Sperling, who has poured millions of dollars into research for the Missyplicity Project. The project began as an attempt to clone Sperling's much-loved mongrel dog Missy. Sadly, Missy died in 2002, but gene-banking technology means that her DNA is available for cloning when it becomes possible. So far, cloning a cat has proved simpler than cloning a dog, but research continues. As news of the Missyplicity Project spread, requests came in from people all over the world who wanted to clone their own beloved pets. Although it costs many thousands of dollars, cat cloning is now available—and it is thought that dog cloning will be before too long.

A Dog's Life

A seven-year-old boy was raised by a dog in a remote part of Siberia after being abandoned by his parents at the age of three months. When he was found in August 2001 he couldn't talk and had canine traits like walking on all fours, and growling.

In the Dog-house

When Cora the tiger cub was born in a circus in France, her mother didn't have enough milk to feed her. So she was adopted by a kindly Pointer called Diane.

I Smell a Cat

The case against a drug suspect in Waterloo, Iowa, was dismissed in 2003 because the police sniffer-dog had failed to complete the search. The highly trained dog had abandoned its duty in order to chase a passing cat.

Doggy Bag

Canadian inventor Paul Le Fevre has come up with a dual-purpose "doggy bag." Although it has a compartment for dog food, it is essentially a designer diaper for dogs so that dog owners can keep the streets clean.

Andy Warhol

Jacqui Adams is the proud owner of the world's fastest ferret, Warhol. At the 1999 North of England Ferret Racing Championships, Warhol sped 32 ft (10 m) in 12.59 seconds.

Ready, Steady, Slow!

It was a nail-biting finish at the 2004 World Championship Snail Race, as the snails lined up for a life-changing race for fame. The prize-winning mollusk was Owen, who stole the show with a record time, to the delight of his trainer, eight-year-old Joe Clarke from Norfolk, England. Snails secrete mucus from a special gland that enables them to slide on one foot, and they can apparently reach speeds of between 0.029 and .0063 mph (0.013 and 0.0028 m/sec).

It took Owen a full 2 minutes, 10 seconds to reach the finish line of the 13-in (33-cm) course.

Asking for Trouble

Trouble, a six-year-old beagle, recently set his paw prints in concrete when he was honored with a place in the Canine World Heroes Walk of Fame. Trouble is a star in the canine world, because he managed to sniff out 1.3 million lb (590,000 kg) of illegal drugs and $27.9 million of drug money in 2003.

Bear Necessities

In 2004, a paralyzed Colorado man lay in bed unable to do anything while a 500-lb (227-kg) bear spent two hours ransacking his kitchen for snacks. Known in the area as "Fat Albert," the black bear helped himself to 4 lb (2 kg) of chocolate. Wildlife agents later found Albert sleeping off his sugar high in the man's dining room.

He'll Have You in Stitches

Baggio, a nine-year-old cockatiel, has stunned his tailor owner, Jack Territo, by learning to sew! The British bird learned his craft by mimicking his owner.

A Feather in Her Cap

In 1947, Beverly Bell spent five hours creating this dress made entirely from turkey feathers. It's not just the dress that is made from feathers, the shoes are also made from quill ends.

Ratty and Mole

Moles were causing a real problem in Lincolnshire, England, but when a man decided to hunt for them using his car headlights he wished he hadn't bothered. He crashed the car into his house, the fuel tank exploded, and his home burned to the ground.

Heavy Vetting

Americans spend more than six billion dollars per year on vets' fees.

Shrine to Swine

Outside a bungalow in Houston, Texas, are signs such as "No Porking," and "Pignic Area." A "pigup" truck stands in the driveway and the mailbox is shaped like a pig. The house is Pigdom—owner Victoria Herberta's own hog heaven. Victoria has had a lifelong fascination with pigs, particularly the famous Priscilla, which she taught to swim and sometimes shared a bed with. In 1984, Priscilla rescued a boy from drowning, leading to the creation of a "Priscilla the Pig Day" in Houston in the animal's honor. Although no longer allowed to keep pigs in the city, Victoria's devotion to them endures. "Pigs are intelligent, loving, and sensitive," she says. "I adore them."

Pet Dating

An internet dating agency in the U.K. offers to find companions for dogs—and possibly for their owners as well.

Costume Drama

Dog-owners in Nunoa, Chile, have started a trend of dressing their pets in fancy costumes when taking them for a walk. Dogs about town have been seen dressed as Batman and Robin, Easter bunnies, Cinderella, and Snow White. For more formal occasions, they have even been known to wear tuxedos or wedding dresses!

Steeple Chase

The Dog Chapel, East St. Johnsbury, Vermont, looks like an ordinary white clapboard church—except for the winged dog on the steeple, the stained-glass windows featuring canine characters, and the photographs commemorating dead pets on the walls.

Big Shot

A Michigan man shot at an opossum in his kitchen, but hit a gas line, causing an explosion that caused $45,000 worth of damage.

Frog Match

Frog Fantasies is an unusual museum in Eureka Springs, Arkansas. It features nothing but frogs made from porcelain, wood, majolica, jade, coconut, cedar roots, and just about anything else you can think of.

Bundle of Fluff

Crystal is the biggest rabbit in the world, according to her owner Sue Dooley. The bumper British bunny weighs in at a whopping 27 lb (12 kg).

Groom Service

Luxury pet hotels offer condos and penthouse suites for dogs and cats, complete with ceiling fans and televisions. At PETSuites Pet Resort, pampered pets can also receive grooming and play sessions for an extra charge.

Spiraling Starlings

No one knows why 300 dead starlings dropped out of the sky in Tacoma, Washington, in 1998. One theory suggests that they were blown to earth by a violent gust of wind.

Lore and Order

Folklore says you can predict the severity of a winter by the coat of the woolly worm, a black and brown caterpillar, in fall. But Jim Morton was confused by their different colors and felt the only way of deciding which worm was right was to hold a race. So each year since 1977, Banner Elk, North Carolina, hosts the Woolly Worm Festival, and the winning worm is the official weather forecaster.

The Lamb and the Unicorn
Both the two-headed lamb and the unicorn were discovered by John Turner of Haddon-on-the-Wall, England.

Ripley's®
TWO-HEADED LAMB
EXHIBIT NO: 19546
BORN WITH TWO HEADS ON A FARM IN ENGLAND

Ripley's®
UNICORN LAMB
EXHIBIT NO: 19421
HAD A HORN STICKING OUT OF ITS HEAD, WHICH MADE IT LOOK LIKE A UNICORN

Coffin-bearer

In a record-breaking stunt, John Lamedica from Delaware lay down in a Plexiglas coffin… with more than 20,000 giant Madagascan hissing cockroaches to keep him company.

Cat Suits

A Japanese website offers tailor-made cat costumes to dress up your pet. Your cat could be a chick, a frog or, strangely, Anne of Green Gables.

It Sticks out a Mile
Phoebe, a Malaysian giant stick insect, is the world's longest bug, measuring a massive 18 in (45 cm).

Croc Climbing

A 13-ft (4-m) crocodile attempted to drag a man from his tent in Queensland, Australia, but was prevented from doing so by a daring 60-year-old woman who jumped on its back. Eventually, someone shot the crocodile.
The man and woman both had to be treated for broken bones.

I Smell a Rat

Scientists at the University of Florida have identified neural signals that are transmitted by rats when they locate a scent. This means that eventually the rodents could be used to help in rescue attempts.

MaKe Yourself at Home

BAILEY D. BUFFALO spends more time in his owner's kitchen than in his shed!

Jim and Linda Sautner of Alberta, Canada, raised the buffalo from infancy, hence its tame nature. Bailey weighs 1,650 lb (748 kg), but visits the Sautner house every day.

Bailey D. Buffalo enjoys privileges not usually experienced by buffalo— he's allowed into his owner's kitchen, although he rarely dines with them.

Ten-year-old Carissa Boulden watches her pet horse, Princess, eat a plate of spaghetti at the family's dining table in Sydney, Australia. Princess is even allowed to drink beer on Sundays!

The Lion in Winter
In 2003, Leon the "house lion" kept Radka Sarkanyova and her teddy bear company in the Czech Republic.

27

The World's Smartest Dog

Chanda-Leah, from Ontario, Canada, is officially the cleverest pooch in the world. She is an 11 year-old poodle that has amassed a repertoire of more than 1,000 tricks, including skateboarding, playing the piano, and untying shoelaces. She and her owner, Sharon Robinson, have performed on TV and toured North America. The performing poodle is also potty trained, and can respond to numerous verbal and hand commands.

Chanda-Leah visits between 150 and 200 hospitals, schools, and nursing homes each year, entertaining everyone with her talented trickery.

Gator Aid

Matthew Goff didn't hesitate to stab a 6-ft (1.8-m) alligator in the eye with his pocket knife after it attempted to nab his puppy, Sugar. When she was off her leash, Sugar wandered to the edge of the pond, and the alligator took the opportunity to grab her head. Fortunately for 29-year-old Matthew, jabbing the reptile in its eye was the right move. Sugar managed to scamper home, with only three teeth marks to show for her near-death experience.

A Meaty Treat

A Moscow company makes meat-based birthday cakes for dogs. They cost about $60.

Bark 'n' Boots

Police in Northumbria, England, are issuing their police dogs boots to protect their paws. Police officers think they will prove especially useful in crime scenes where there is glass on the floor.

A Taste of Her Own Medicine

Dr. Perez's patients include people—and their pets. At her practice in Santiago, Chile, she uses alternative medicine to treat conditions such as stress and depression.

The Flying Dachshund

A miniature dachshund called Brutus holds the world record for the highest canine sky-dive: 15,000 ft (4,600 m). Brutus, who lives in California, has made more than 70 sky-dives.

Pup in a Cup

Weighing just 1 lb (450 g) and standing just 4 in (10 cm) tall, Star the Chihuahua stopped growing at just five weeks old. Though she is small, she is still perfectly formed.

Ripley's®

PIG HAIR BALL
EXHIBIT NO: 6403
MEASURING MORE THAN 18 IN (46 CM)
IN CIRCUMFERENCE

What a Choker
Pig hair balls are very rough and spikey. Because pigs cannot vomit their hair balls, they can only be found when the animal dies.

Great Balls of Fur
Ripley employee Lisa Shea held the two winning hair balls in the 1994 contest to find the largest hair ball in America. The winning balls were submitted by Mike Canchola of Colorado.

Zebra's Crossing
The second Baron Rothschild had a collection of exotic animals at his home in Buckinghamshire, England, in the late 19th century. It included kangaroos, a dingo, giant tortoises, and a team of four zebras that pulled his carriage.

Trunk Call
The Alaska Zoo in Anchorage is building what it believes to be the world's first elephant treadmill. The zoo-keepers need the machine because their 9,120-lb (4,137-kg) elephant, Maggie, is a tad lazy. The final cost of the treadmill could be as much as $250,000.

Neck and Neck
While it is commonly known that the giraffe is the tallest animal in the world, sometimes reaching heights in excess of 18 ft (5.5 m), did you know that it has a tongue that is more than 1 ft (30 cm) long? That means giraffes can lick their own ears!

Ripley's®

COW HAIR BALLS
EXHIBIT NO: 6617
THESE WINNING HAIR BALLS ARE 34 IN
(83 CM) IN CIRCUMFERENCE

bad FeatheR day

WHIPPER THE BUDGIE suffers from the bird version of a bad hair day, every day of his life. Born with a rare genetic mutation called "Feather Duster," Whipper was hand-reared by owner Julie Hayward after his parents rejected him.

Not only was he shunned by his own parents—Charles and Camilla—but also by other birds who live in the same New Zealand aviary. The story has a happy ending though, because Whipper now attracts an endless stream of visitors at his new home.

There have been only three cases of the "feather duster" syndrome recorded in the last 60 years.

Feathered Friend

After terrorizing the residents of Holland, Michigan, for months during 2001, a turkey with a fowl attitude was driven out of town. The aggressive bird had pinned people in their cars or behind their front doors, and menaced any pedestrians who crossed his path.

Love of Faith

An Oregon man's lost dog was found after an extensive search that lasted two months and involved four psychics and one white witch. The day after the owner got his German shepherd back, the pet-sitter who had been looking after the dog when it went missing, was sued by him for $160,000.

Grin and Bear It

A Romanian shepherd was fleeing from a bear when he slipped and broke his leg. He was rescued by his Pekinese dog, who lured the bear away before returning to its injured owner.

What's Your Poison?

Police were called to an Austrian snake trader's home, but when they got there the man tried to attack them with two poisonous snakes. However, both the cobras bit the snake trader, who then had to be taken to hospital to be injected with an antidote.

Wild Cards

Exotic pets, including two macaque monkeys, a moose, and a raccoon, were seized by police from the home of a millionaire from Alberta, Canada. Apparently, the monkeys, Tarzan and Jane, used to play cards with the family.

The Camel's Got the Hump

Jewel, a 1,600-lb (726-kg) aging Bactrian camel at the Brookfield Zoo in Illinois, suffered such arthritis in her front legs that she was nearly lame. However, that's all changed thanks to acupuncture. She's not happy about the needles though, and since camels can kick in any direction, doctors must be nimble during Jewel's treatments.

Playing Chicken

A British turkey avoided death at Christmas by becoming the surrogate father of some chicken's eggs that were due to hatch.

Mighty Mastiff
Hercules, an English mastiff, who lives with his owner in the U.S.A., weighs a staggering 282 lb (128 kg). The hefty hound entered the record books as the world's largest dog.

Biting Back

A 65-year-old man who was fishing off the coast of Georgia was more than a little shocked when a 30-lb (14-kg) barracuda jumped into his boat and bit him. Apparently, the fish leaped 30 ft (9 m) from the water, as if it had wings, and proceeded to latch on to his finger. The man had to be treated at a hospital for the serious cut.

Drive Time

While his owner watched Canada win the 2004 World Hockey Cup, a dog managed to put a truck into gear and coast down a hill in Whitehorse, Yukon Territory. A man out for a walk alerted police after seeing the vehicle pass with a black Labrador Retriever at the wheel.

Rooster Boosters

Organizers of the 2001 New Mexico State Fair Rooster-crowing Contest blamed a quiet event on the heat. Spectators and owners flapped and clucked like chickens in a bid to stimulate activity, but the standard was so low that the winning rooster only had to crow twice.

Bubble Trouble

Connie Beck woke one morning in 2000 to hear strange noises in her home in Howard, Pennsylvania. Upon investigation, she found a deer taking a bubble bath in the bath tub! The deer had not only gained entry to the house, it had also managed to turn on the bathroom tap and knock over the bottle of bubble bath.

Faith Healer

Faith, a Labrador/Chow cross, was born without her two front legs and seemed destined to be destroyed. She was saved by Oklahoma City civil servant Jude Stringfellow, and has never looked back. Not only has she mastered the art of walking on two legs like a human being, but she has also become a celebrity—with her own agent, lawyer, and even a part in the latest *Harry Potter* movie.

Hopping Mad

U.S. judge Randy Anglen was reported to be seeking compensation in 2004 after finding a dead mouse in a bottle of beer at his home in Hollister, Missouri. He had drunk the beer by the time he saw the rodent.

Slip into a Nice Bath

German angler Paul Richter doesn't have a rubber duck in his bath—he has been sharing the tub with a giant eel for the past 35 years. When he first caught the slippery creature, his children refused to allow him to cook and eat it. Although his children have now left home, Paul and his wife have become so fond of "Eelfie" that the intended supper has become a family pet that often joins them in the bath.

Can You Dig It?

After being hit by a mail delivery truck, Sweetie the dog showed no signs of life. Distraught owner Glenda Stevens dug a grave and buried her pet in the garden of her home in Park Hills, Missouri. However, hours later she was amazed to see Sweetie's hind legs sticking out of the ground. The dog, which had suffered a broken leg and jaw, was digging itself out of its own grave!

Do You Take This Dog...

After a "love at first sight" meeting while they were being walked by their owners, Saul, a Labrador guide dog, married Foxy, a Border Collie in August 2004 at a ceremony organized by Hollywood Hounds. The groom's best man looked on in awe as the bride made her entrance—traditionally late of course—accompanied by bridesmaids Misty, Cara, and Rena. The happy couple's marriage was then blessed by a vicar.

Committed canines Foxy and Saul had 35 guests at their wedding, including the traditional best man and bridesmaids.

On His Last Legs
Boontawee Siengwong, of Bangkok, Thailand, spent 28 days and nights eating and sleeping with 1,000 centipedes in a glass room measuring just 129 sq ft (12 sq m).

Make It Snappy

When Erroberto Piza Rios fancies a game of soccer, he chooses opponents who have a tendency to snap—his pet crocodiles. Errober to delights tourists on the beach at Iztapa, Mexico, by kicking a ball around with the reptiles, all of which are named after former soccer stars. His favorite trick is to place the ball on one of their heads so that they can lift their powerful jaws and let it roll down their back. He claims never to have been attacked and, in another demonstration, intrigues onlookers by allowing a small crocodile to bite his face gently.

A Day They'll Never Forget

Two pairs of elephants were married in a lavish Valentine's Day ceremony in Ayuthaya, Thailand, in 2001. The elephants wore gowns embroidered with red hearts and even had their trunks brightly painted for the occasion.

The Odd Couple

An orphaned baby hippopotamus has adopted a 100-year-old tortoise as its surrogate mother. The hippo, Owen, which weighs about 650 lb (300 kg), follows the giant tortoise everywhere, and becomes angry and protective whenever the tortoise is approached. They live together at an animal facility in Mombasa, Kenya, Africa.

On All Fours
This cockerel was born in Tirana, Albania, with four legs.

InDex

ACKNOWLEDGMENTS

Jacket (t/r) Rex Features

6 (b) Paul Cooper/Rex Features; 7 (t/c) Rex Features, (c) Drew Gardner/Rex Features; 8 (t/l, t/c, t/r) Mike Walker/Rex Features; 9 (c) Leon Schadeberg/Rex Features, (b) Masatoshi Okauchi/Rex Features; 10 Issei Kato/Reuters; 13 (t/l) Kimimasa Mayama/Reuters, (b) Alex Grimm/Reuters; 14 (b) Reuters; 15 (t/r) Simon Kwong/Reuters, (c) HO/Reuters; 16 (b) Mark Campbell/Rex Features; 17 (t/r, c) Andy Newman/AFP/Getty Images; 18 John Chapple/Rex Features, (b/r) AFP/Getty Images; 19 (t/l) Paul Jones/AFP/Getty Images, (b) Simon Baker/Reuters; 22 (b) Getty Images; 23 (t) Paul Cooper/Rex Features, (b) EDPPics/Usher/Rex Features; 24 (b) Rex Features; 25 (b) Phil Yeomans/Rex Features; 26 (b/c) Alisdair Macdonald/Rex Features; 27 (t/r) Tim Wimborne/Reuters, (c) Dan Riedlhuber/Reuters, (c/l) Rex Features; 28 (t/c, t/r) Courtesy of Sharon Robinson, (b/r) John O Reilley/Rex Features; 30 Rex Features; 31 Kevin Wisniewski/Rex Features; 32 (b) Paul Nicholls/Rex Features; 33 (t/l) Sukree Sukplang/Reuters, (b) Reuters.

All other photos are from Ripley's Entertainment Inc.
Every attempt has been made to acknowledge correctly and contact copyright holders and we apologize in advance for any unintentional errors or omissions, which will be corrected in future editions.